Native American
Medicine

TAMRA ORR

Senior Consulting Editor Dr. Troy Johnson
Professor of History and American Indian Studies
California State University

MASON CREST PUBLISHERS • PHILADELPHIA

NATIVE AMERICAN LIFE

NATIVE AMERICAN LIFE

$\mathcal{N}$ative $\mathcal{A}$merican
Medicine

TAMRA ORR

Senior Consulting Editor Dr. Troy Johnson
Professor of History and American Indian Studies
California State University

MASON CREST PUBLISHERS • PHILADELPHIA

NATIVE AMERICAN LIFE

Mason Crest Publishers
370 Reed Road
Broomall, PA 19008
www.masoncrest.com

First printing

1 3 5 7 9 8 6 4 2

Library of Congress Cataloging-in-Publication Data
on file at the Library of Congress

ISBN 1-59084-119-0

Frontispiece: Old Bear, a medicine man, poses with some of his tools in this painting by George Catlin. Medicine men used religious, magical, and herbal cures, as well as common sense treatments.

On the cover: An Inuit shaman's mask is pictured on the front cover, while the image on the back cover is a Haida or Tsimshian ceremonial rattle with a T'kul face and frogs.

Table of Contents

Introduction

For hundreds of years the dominant image of the Native American has been that of a stoic warrior, often wearing a full-length eagle feather headdress, riding a horse in pursuit of the buffalo, or perhaps surrounding some unfortunate wagon train filled with innocent west-bound American settlers. Unfortunately there has been little written or made available to the general public to dispel this erroneous generalization. This misrepresentation has resulted in an image of native people that has been translated into books, movies, and television programs that have done little to look deeply into the native worldview, cosmology, and daily life. Not until the 1990 movie *Dances with Wolves* were native people portrayed as having a human persona. For the first time, native people could express humor, sorrow, love, hate, peace, and warfare. For the first time native people could express themselves in words other than "ugh" or "Yes, Kemo Sabe." This series has been written to provide a more accurate and encompassing journey into the world of the Native Americans.

When studying the native world of the Americas, it is extremely important to understand that there are few "universals" that apply across tribal boundaries. With over 500 nations and 300 language groups the worlds of the Native Americans were diverse. The traditions of one group may or may not have been shared by neighboring groups. Sports, games, dance, subsistence patterns, clothing, and religion differed—greatly in some instances. And although nearly all native groups observed festivals and ceremonies necessary to insure the renewal of their worlds, these too varied greatly.

Of equal importance to the breaking down of old myopic and stereotypic images is that the authors in this series credit Native

Americans with a sense of agency. Contrary to the views held by the Europeans who came to North and South America and established the United States, Canada, Mexico, and other nations, some Native American tribes had sophisticated political and governing structures— that of the member nations of the Iroquois League, for example. Europeans at first denied that native people had religions but rather "worshiped the devil," and demanded that Native Americans abandon their religions for the Christian worldview. The readers of this series will learn that native people had well-established religions, led by both men and women, long before the European invasion began in the 16th and 17th centuries.

Gender roles also come under scrutiny in this series. European settlers in the northeastern area of the present-day United States found it appalling that native women were "treated as drudges" and forced to do the men's work in the agricultural fields. They failed to understand, as the reader will see, that among this group the women owned the fields and scheduled the harvests. Europeans also failed to understand that Iroquois men were diplomats and controlled over one million square miles of fur-trapping area. While Iroquois men sat at the governing council, Iroquois clan matrons caucused with tribal members and told the men how to vote.

These are small examples of the material contained in this important series. The reader is encouraged to use the extended bibliographies provided with each book to expand his or her area of specific interest.

Dr. Troy Johnson
Professor of History and American Indian Studies
California State University

1 Medicine Men to the Rescue

The sound of the women crying could be heard for what seemed like miles. All eyes were focused on the young boy lying motionless on the ground, a bullet hole in his shoulder. His eyes were closed and his breathing was slow. The chief knew that no simple **herb** or tea was going to cure this child. Instead, help from the Great Spirit was needed.

"Send for the Buffalo Doctors!" shouted the tribe's chief.

The boy was rolled onto an animal-skin robe and carried carefully into the chief's tepee. Time crawled by as everyone listened for the sound of horses' hooves hammering across the golden prairie. Soon, a low rumble was heard, and the Indians could see the Buffalo Doctors of the Omaha Buffalo Society galloping towards them, long, black hair trailing down their bare, tanned backs.

Within minutes, all of the doctors were sitting

A Native American medicine man waves a rattle in order to frighten evil spirits away and heal a member of his tribe in this 19th-century illustration. Healers were among the most important and revered members of Native American tribes.

This Crow medicine bundle was made by wrapping an eagle's body in cloth. Straps were attached so the bundle could be suspended over a sick person during rituals. The Crow healer who made this bundle probably chose to use an eagle after seeing the bird in a vision. Native Americans believed that eagles were a source of great power.

on the ground around the injured boy. For quite a while, no one spoke at all. The doctors were certainly there in body, but their minds seemed far away. Finally, in a soft voice, one doctor spoke to the crowd.

"I have had a vision of our great protector, the Buffalo," he said. "He has told me the special secret of medicine and song that is needed to heal this boy."

He began to sing a song known only by himself. Next, he pulled some roots out from the medicine bundle worn around his neck. He started chewing on them and then gulped a drink of water to make the roots softer.

Suddenly, the doctor stood and began to paw the ground and make loud snorting noises like a buffalo. He circled the boy several times and then drew in a big breath. He took aim and blew the root and water mixture right into the open wound.

11

For four long days, this same procedure continued. Four was a sacred number to the tribe, and so it was with great relief that, at the end of the fourth day, the boy opened his eyes. The Buffalo Doctors rose and began to sing a song of triumph, then went to collect their reward. Horses, robes, bear claw necklaces, and eagle feathers were given in gratitude by the tribe, and the Buffalo Doctors rode off, once again having conquered the demons and evil spirits. The boy would recover completely and live a long and rich life.

Far away, in another Indian village, another healing process was taking place. The Mescalero Apache tribe had called on their *shaman* for help. One of the tribe members was on the ground, obviously in pain. Nothing

This shaman's rattle is shaped to depict a bird called an oyster catcher, which carries a family of otters on its back. The rattle's purpose was to cure mental illness, because otters were believed to have the ability to cause insanity.

the others had done had helped. The songs and chants didn't seem to make a difference, and so, finally, the shaman had been summoned to come and talk to the *supernatural* world before this man died.

Anxious faces looked on as the medicine man circled around the sick man. He shook his medicine bag, then grabbed a hollowed-out horn, covered with carvings, out of it. He walked over to the man on the ground and pushed the horn against the top of his patient's head. Minutes passed. The only sound was the soft breathing of the shaman and the loud groans of the man.

With a sudden yell of victory, the shaman stood up, arms overhead. In his right hand was a blue, three-inch long bone. It had a red tip and was shaped like an arrow. Four human hairs were wrapped around the bone.

"He is cured!" cried the shaman. "This bone was placed inside his head as a weapon by an angry witch and he was near death, but now he shall live!"

The village erupted into a cry of happiness and relief, even though the man was still on the ground, moaning. The medicine man took the gifts that were showered upon him from all directions and then, in silence, headed back to his tepee set far off from the village, alone as a shaman should be.

Native Americans have an incredibly rich history that spans hundreds of years and crosses the globe from Canada to the Caribbean. Their beliefs about sickness and medicine are steeped in legend, religion, and an amazing knowledge of the earth's many gifts. While some of the methods they used to heal may seem odd or silly, others may sound familiar because they are still used today in one form or another. ⑤

13

NATIVE AMERICAN LIFE

2. The Native American Philosophy of Medicine

Do you know what different things can make a person sick? Native Americans of the past were not truly aware of the major causes of illness: germs and viruses or poor nutrition, for example. They knew that simple sicknesses like a cold or cough, or even a more serious injury like a broken bone, could be taken care of by using the gifts the earth provided. they also believed that other illnesses were due to a problem from the supernatural world, where demons, gods, and the Great Spirit lived. To the Native Americans, disease was a mystery, and anything that was mysterious was treated in the same way as something that was holy or sent from the Great Spirit.

The Shoshone, a Great Plains tribe, believed that illness was due to a ghost living inside the body; while the Tlingit tribe of the Pacific Northwest

A medicine man practices sacred rituals used to protect the soul of a dying member of the tribe. The mystery and secrecy surrounding medicine men and their healing rituals gave them an aura of spiritual power.

This 17th-century drawing by Jacques le Moyne shows the various methods employed by the natives of Florida to treat their sick. One man reclines while women suck blood from a slit on his forehead. The man on the right breathes in the smoke from burning seeds, while at the center of the illustration another man smokes tobacco, which was believed to have healing properties.

thought that illness came from evil spirits. Others felt that disease was a punishment sent for angering the gods, loss of a soul, or the failure to perform a *ritual* or ceremony properly. Another Great Plains tribe called the Assiniboines believed that if a person was in a coma or unconscious, it might be because his spirit had decided to travel east. Only a holy man could bring it back safely. If the patient awoke, the trip was successful. If he did not wake up or if he died, it was a failure. The Cheyenne believed that illness was due either to offending special, powerful spirits, like Owl or Coyote, or to acts of witchcraft

Certain tribes from the Pacific Northwest believed that before babies were born, they lived in a wonderful place called "Babyland." Only babies lived there, and they spent all day playing. After they were born, if they liked life on earth they stayed. If they didn't like it, however, they would die so that they could return to play in Babyland. If a baby became ill, he or she was kept far away from the other babies on the chance that he or she might try to convince them to return to Babyland also.

Indian mothers would take great care of their new babies, bathing them daily, rubbing them with whale oil, and powdering them with willow ash before bundling them up in cedar-bark diapers. In some tribes, for the first year of life, babies were carried on their mother's backs on a cradleboard made of hollowed-out cedar wood. This kept the baby close to its mother at all times and out of harm's way.

17

and ghosts. The Windway medicine men of the Apache and Navajo tribes felt that stomach sicknesses came from snakes; while others in the tribe believed illness was brought on by thunder and lightning.

A group of Native American healers beat a ceremonial drum. The drum was a common element of healing rituals. The round shape of the instrument represented the wholeness of the universe, while the drum's constant beat was a symbol of the beat of the heart of the Great Spirit.

There was little to no separation between daily life and the spiritual world for Native Americans. Most of them believed spirits were found everywhere, in the sky, earth, mountains, rivers, and in every animal. It's easy to understand, with this many different spirits all around, how one might get offended in one way or another.

Because most tribes felt that serious illnesses came from the spirit world, they needed a doctor who would be able to contact this world and thus find just the right cure. While they went by many different names, these special doctors were looked at as a link between the real world and the supernatural, and their tribes honored them. Within a tribe, healers often were second in rank only to the chief. §

3 Shamans, Medicine Men, and Other Healers

Chances are that when you go into a medical office in search of a way to feel better, you see a person that you usually call "doctor." Native Americans had many different names for their healers. These names include diviner, prophet, healer, herbalist, shaman, and medium. Each one of these names translates into something similar to doctor or priest. Whatever the healer was called, however, he was the person to whom the entire tribe turned to communicate directly with the spirit world and thus help cure those who were suffering from an illness sent from unhappy or evil spirits. Not only could these special people heal, they were also often looked to for predicting the future, casting spells, protection from enemies, and influencing the weather. Some shamans were able to make out-of-body trips that they

Native Americans often painted their bodies with special "medicine" designs before dances or battles. The application of the paint was intended as protection. The mystical beliefs of Native Americans were encouraged by the medicine men, who needed the faith of the people in order to succeed as healers.

This is a bear claw medicine token, used by the Crow people. Artifacts like this were used in conjunction with face and body paint and ritual songs to ensure the presence of the "Sacred Helper." It was probably worn as a personal ornament by a warrior in battle.

took in search of food, and then they would direct the hunters to that place they had seen on their journeys. Among the Jivaro Indians of Ecuador, where one in every four men was a shaman, the medicine men even worked occasionally as spies. They would be asked to check up on someone through an out-of-body trip to make sure they were behaving properly. Sometimes, they were even used to locate missing objects or to "see" a crime so that the people of the village knew who to blame for it. These shamans were much like a minister, magician, and physician all rolled up into one person.

How did someone become a medicine man or shaman? It wasn't an easy process. It often began either right after a period of *fasting* and experiencing a special dream or vision. In this dream, the person would often see an animal—like a bear or a bird—that would tell him of his new power and how to use it for the good of the tribe. In some southwestern tribes, these visions may have been brought on by the use of certain plants, especially the *peyote* cactus, which, when eaten, is strong enough to cause people to have *hallucinations*. An Inuit shaman told Danish Arctic explorer Knud Rasmussen what it was like to go

through such an experience. "I could see and hear in a totally different way," he said. "I had gained *enlightenment*, the shaman's light of brain and body."

The skill or ability to be a shaman tended to run in families, and children would sometimes know at an early age if they were going to follow the shaman tradition. If a child was moody or tended to daydream a lot, the tribe might suspect he would grow up to be a

Lakota Sioux spiritual leaders take part in a peyote ritual on the Rosebud reservation in South Dakota. The peyote cactus contains a drug called mescaline, which causes hallucinogenic sensations when eaten.

Were there female Native American healers? While they were rare, they did exist. One of the most famous was Sanapia, a Comanche Eagle Doctor born in 1895. She continued to practice healing until her death in 1969. She used many different herbs to treat everything from insect bites to epilepsy.

shaman. It was even said within some tribes that if a young person heard a voice calling during sleep and woke up to see a mouse disappearing, he would probably grow up to be a medicine man. The mouse was thought to be the only animal that could speak all languages and was often considered the messenger of the Great Spirit.

After that first vision, a medicine man's training would officially begin. The training could last from just a few months to several years. The *initiate* would learn the songs, chants, spells, and dances he had seen in his dreams, and would gather items for his medicine bundle, the bag he usually wore around his neck to carry some of his "tools of the trade." A recently discovered medicine bundle from the Winnebago tribe contained items common in medicine bundles, such as bear paws, animal bones, skins, furs, bird heads, wooden bowls, spoons, and precious stones, like turquoise and green *malachite*. In addition, medicine men also searched out their own power objects, such as magical stones and charms. They made rattles out of *gourds*, animal bladders, deer hooves, furs, and eagles' heads. They carved and painted masks to wear, and constructed a variety of drums, fans, and spears. Just

25

NATIVE AMERICAN LIFE

as importantly, they used this time to learn about the different plants of the earth and how they could best be used for healing.

While these special people were honored within a tribe, medicine men also led rather difficult lives. They had much to learn. In just one healing ceremony, they might sing as many as 80 chants, each one with as many as 30 verses. Can you imagine trying to memorize the words to that many songs? In addition, they often were not allowed to marry and had to live alone and isolated. Even worse, if the shaman wasn't able to cure a person, not only did he not get paid, he was sometimes beaten or even killed.

A shaman wasn't always called when a person became sick or injured. Instead, the villagers would wait and see if simple remedies would help. If they didn't, the medicine man was called upon. The

In the northeast, the tribes of the Iroquois Confederacy had a special group of healers they called "False Faces." These men wore unique masks representing several of the different powerful spirits. The masks were carved on the trunk of a live tree and then carefully cut out. If the masks were created in the morning hours, they were painted red; if they were created in the evening hours, they were painted black. A mask that took an entire day to make was painted both colors. Twisted bark strips were used for hair, and the mask was rubbed with oil and then sprinkled with tobacco to show respect for it. The "False Faces" were always made up of men who had once been sick themselves and, while recovering, were given the knowledge of how to become healers.

27

Members of the Iroquois False Face Society wore masks like this one, carved from a living tree. In spring and fall they went from house to house, shaking turtle-shell rattles and chanting to drive away the demons of disease.

ceremonies and tools would vary from tribe to tribe, but most followed the same basic pattern. Many shamans would start by preparing themselves to heal by spending much time in **meditation** and prayer. They felt this was a way to stop thinking about themselves and focus instead on what the Great Spirit wanted them to do.

A number of the medicine men would begin their healing ceremonies by going into a **trance** to connect with the spirit world and to help "see" inside their patients' bodies. They would bring out their chants, spells, and songs; they would shake their gourds, paint their faces, and bang their drums. Next, they might set out their essential tools, such as jointed puppets, skulls, and carved boxes. They would use the herbs they thought were most needed for this particular condition, often chewing them up, mixing them with water, and then spitting the mixture into the wound or over the painful body part. Now and then, the shamans would use tobacco smoke as part of the healing process, blowing it into the ears, mouth, and nose of the sick person to try and drive out the demons inside.

Native American healers believed that a person's health is tied to more than just his or her physical condition. The person's mental and spiritual condition is important as well. Today, this belief in treating the whole person has evolved into a medical philosophy and practice that are becoming more widely accepted, called holistic medicine.

Shamans were often feared by the people of their tribes. When a shaman of the Tlingit tribe died, the tribe would put his body on a board in a separate grave house, and no one was to come near it. In fact, they believed that merely drinking from a nearby stream or picking berries in the area was life-threatening. Even his tools were never touched after death. People with a weak guardian spirit stayed far away from the medicine man in case he tried to draw out their souls. When a shaman died in some of the southeast and woodlands tribes, the men and women of the village would show their sadness by fasting and cutting off their hair.

Sometimes, the Native Americans believed, the evil spirits inside of the patient might fly out and attack the shaman, and then he would have to battle them for control of his own soul.

Another procedure that many different medicine men used was one that commonly employed a bit of trickery with it. A typical *diagnosis* for an ill person was that a witch, ghost, or evil spirit had put a foreign object somewhere inside the patient's body. The shaman would go into a trance to figure out where and what the object was and then he would grab a horn, pipe stem, or tube and appear to suck it out of the person. He would hold up the object triumphantly to show the others that he had succeeded.

A Crow Indian named Bull All The Time has gone down in history as curing a number of people in this manner. According to legend, he sucked a bone, a black beetle, and a piece of meat out of his

29

NATIVE AMERICAN LIFE

patients. Other shamans might suck at a spot on the patient and then either belch or vomit to show they had removed the problem.

It wasn't uncommon for a shaman to have one of these so-called foreign objects stuck up his sleeve or in his mouth to prove that he had really done his job. He might also bite his own tongue or make a small cut on the patient's skin so that when he stood up, there would be blood on his lips. Considering that some medicine men might be killed if they didn't cure the patient, it is not surprising that they occasionally resorted to cheating a little bit.

Other tribes used different methods. Ute medicine men drove out evil spirits by stretching the patient out on the ground and cutting him with an eagle claw from head to foot, while Blackfeet shamans would spray yellow paint on the patient by blowing it through the hollow wing bones of eagles.

Today, a doctor sends a bill for his services. In Native American tribes, the successful shaman would also be greatly rewarded for his skills and hard work. If he wasn't paid, he would have the right to put back the evil spirit or object. Instead of paying him in money, however, the medicine man often walked away with gifts of horses, food, robes, skins, furs, and other Native American riches.

Why did so many of these ceremonies actually work and make people better? There are three main reasons. The first was that the native people believed strongly in their shaman's power, and that belief was sometimes all it took for them to improve. The mind is strong and if it truly believes that something was done to heal the body, it can actually do a lot on its own to make the body heal. Second, many of the illnesses that shamans were treating were ones that possibly would have gone away in time anyway. Major diseases like *smallpox* weren't around before the arrival of the Europeans in the 16th century, and conditions like a stomachache or headache usually didn't last much longer than a day or so. Third, many of the herbs the shamans used were actually quite effective in stopping pain and illness. S

The northeastern tribes of the Great Lakes region had a medicine society called the Midewiwin. This group of doctors kept their healing and ritual information completely secret. Their medicine bags were usually made of otter skin and decorated with porcupine quills, beads, and ribbon. Members of this society recorded their stories, songs, and remedies by drawing symbols called *pictographs* on scrolls made of birch bark, using sharpened bones for pens. These scrolls are still found today, and they give a glimpse into the different healing methods these tribes used the most.

Among the Hopi tribes of the American southwest, kachina societies performed healing rituals. The Hopi believed that supernatural beings called kachinas served as messengers between gods and humans. Some thought that the kachinas were ancestors of the Pueblo Indians.

Kachinas were believed to live with the Hopi through the winter and spring. They returned to their mountain home in the summer. In July, a festival called Niman was held to celebrate the kachinas' return to the mountains. During the festival, men dressed as kachinas would dance for the tribe. Young children were told that the dancers really were the spirits.

Children were also given kachina dolls, which represented different spirits. The doll in the picture on the opposite page has eyes that represent rain clouds, while the eyelashes symbolize rain.

When Hopi children grew older, they learned about the kachina societies. Some might even become kachina dancers one day. Most of the members of a kachina society were men. A Hopi woman could only join a kachina society if she had been cured by one of the society's rituals.

Native Americans believed that there were natural remedies for all illnesses, and they used plants, berries, and herbs for their healing properties.

4 Using the Earth's Gifts

For basic illnesses or injuries that didn't involve the supernatural world, Native Americans used a wide variety of plants and herbs. Why did they do this? A Cherokee legend probably explains it best. In the old days, so the story goes, all the animals, birds, fishes, and insects could talk to each other. They lived in peace and friendship with the humans for a long time. Then, as the number of humans began to quickly grow, the animals began to run out of room to live. Men invented weapons and killed the animals for skins and food, so the animals decided to protect themselves by introducing diseases to people. The deer chose **rheumatism**, and the fish and reptiles chose loss of appetite. The plant world felt sorry for men, so every tree, bush, and plant, including the grass and the moss, agreed to furnish a remedy for each of the diseases. They said, "I shall appear to help man when he calls upon me in his need." This is how the plant world provided the **antidote** to the illnesses brought on by the vengeful animals. The legend states, "When the doctor is in doubt what treatment to apply for the relief of a patient, the spirit of the plant suggests to him the proper remedy."

Have you ever looked at the plants and flowers growing in your yard and wondered what they would be like to eat? Some taste good, and some don't; some might help you with a health problem, and others might make you extremely sick. Never try a plant in your yard without checking it out with your parents or another adult first, because some simple leaves and beautiful flowers can also be dangerous—even poisonous. Because Native Americans lived in nature, they knew a great deal about the plant world around them and how to

A cherry blossom hangs next to the reddish bark of a cherry tree. Native Americans used the bark of the cherry tree to treat coughing.

NATIVE AMERICAN MEDICINES FOR COMMON HEALTH PROBLEMS

HERB	HEALTH CONDITION
Bee balm	headache, fever
Wintergreen	aching joints
Wild plum	wounds
Elderberry	scrapes, bruises
Goldenrod	sprains, burns
Sumac	sore throats, diarrhea
Witch hazel	sore muscles
Dogbane	earaches
Milkweed	bruises, wounds
Comfrey	ulcers
Echinacea	flu
Raspberry	diarrhea

best use each one. They learned which ones to use mostly through trial and error, and then handed down the information from generation to generation. Sometimes, they would watch sick animals to see what plants they ate. They also spent a great deal of time scouring the forest for unusual plants. To find out if an herb was helpful or not or if it needed to be *diluted*, some of the Native Americans would test them on themselves first to see what happened.

Can you imagine living outdoors in a time period that didn't have suntan lotion and bug repellent? The Indians would rub animal and vegetable oil on their skin to prevent frostbite or sunburn. They would also spread bear grease on their skin to keep bugs off, and some tribes

NATIVE AMERICAN LIFE

used human urine as a shampoo to get rid of lice. The inner bark and needles of **coniferous** trees, like pine, cedar, hemlock, and spruce, were often used for health problems, such as burns, cuts, and sores.

Native Americans did not believe in wasting anything, and the various tribes made sure that they used all parts of a plant: roots, stems, leaves, blossoms, and bark. They were aware of just the right time to pick them also. The inner bark of a tree, for example, was gathered at the beginning of spring when the tree would be full of sap and the bark is easy to remove. Leaves were picked right before a plant blooms, as were the roots of **annual** plants. The roots of **perennial** plants were picked in the autumn. Every time a plant was picked, thanks were given to the earth. Some Native Americans buried treasures in the hole left behind when the plant was uprooted. Others offered tobacco or cornmeal to the plants, Mother Earth, Father Sky, and the four sacred directions: East, West, North, and South. The plants were then used in an amazing number of ways. Sometimes, they were boiled, ground, chewed, or dried and turned into **liniments**, **poultices**, soaps, and teas.

While health conditions like cancer, heart disease, and bacterial illnesses are common today, they weren't then. Instead, health problems

According to Apache legend, when the god Yusn set up the world, he created all plants at the same time. He gave each one of them a purpose—not just the ones that are good to eat. For many, he gave them the ability to act as medicine so that nothing would ever be wasted.

These plants, which can be found at high
altitudes in the deserts of the American
southwest, were used by Native American tribes
for both medicinal and ceremonial purposes.

ranged from accidental injuries to simple illnesses like a sore throat,
cough, toothache, or **arthritis**. Each of these illnesses was treated with a
type of herb—some that worked and some that didn't. A number of
them, however, worked for reasons that can be better understood
today. For example, cherry bark was often used for a cough. Have you
ever noticed that almost all cough syrup today is cherry flavored? This
is because the syrup—just like the bark of the cherry tree—contains a
substance called hydrocyanic acid, and it helps to stop coughing.
Willow bark was often used for fever and pain and it contains salicin,

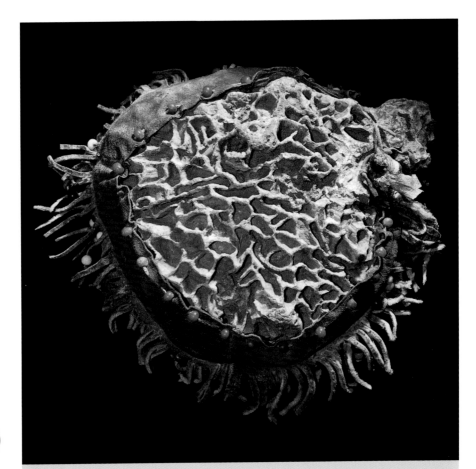

This is an example of "rock medicine" used by the Crow tribe. It would have been kept inside medicine bundles that were opened at the first sound of thunder in spring and just before the onset of winter. The contents were displayed during the "Singing of the Cooked Meat" ceremony, which was intended to bring good fortune to the tribe.

So many different Indian medicines were proven to be effective that one of the most trusted and important medical books, *The U.S. Pharmacopoeia*, includes 170 of them.

one of the main ingredients of aspirin. Have you ever had an ***ointment*** spread on your chest when you have a stuffed-up nose or chest cold? Do you remember what it smelled like? Most likely, that smell came from menthol, which comes from the mint leaves that Native Americans typically used for any kind of ***congestion***. A favorite plant used by tribes was called osha. It has since been proven to be a natural ***antibiotic***.

It was quite a challenge for Native Americans to figure out which plant was best for treating an illness as well as how much, when, and how to take it, but they managed. Thanks to what they learned and handed down, many of the herbs and plants they used are the basis of common medicines today. According to the North Dakota Indian Affairs Commission, Native Americans have given the world over 200 drugs that are now used today for healing, including pain killers, aspirin, the cure for ***malaria***, and the cure for ***scurvy***. ᔕ

41

NATIVE AMERICAN LIFE

This painting by George Catlin
shows the interior of a Native
American sweat lodge during a
ceremony. The sweat lodge was
used by the Indians to cleanse both
their bodies and souls.

5 Other Healing Methods

Beyond the use of medicine men and herbs, what else did Native Americans use for healing? One common treatment was the use of the sweat lodge. This was a dome-shaped building usually made of saplings and twigs with a variety of skins, blankets, or hides as cover. Most sweat lodges were temporary, but some tribes built ones that were made of wood and mud and not meant to be moved. Some southwestern tribes even built sweat lodges that were underground.

Rocks were heated in a fire until they were glowing red, and then they were carefully rolled inside the sweat lodge. Water—sometimes containing crushed herbs—was then poured on the hot rocks to create steam. Many tribe members would sit inside in the incredible heat as long as possible before coming outside and plunging into the nearest cold stream, lake, or river. They felt the process was cleansing for both the body and the soul. Native Americans would use the sweat lodge just before an important ritual or ceremony or if they were feeling troubled. Some tribes made it part of their preparation before sending young members on a *vision quest*. Older members would also use it for relief from the pains of arthritis and rheumatism.

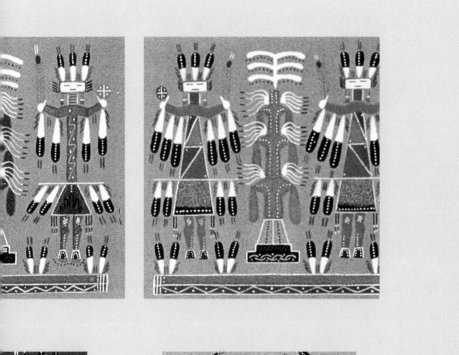

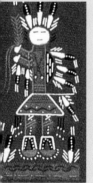

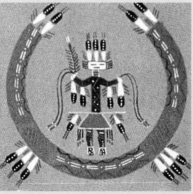

45

These are examples of Navajo sand paintings. Large
sand paintings were often used as part of healing
ceremonies.

Native American tribe members perform a stomp dance to help a sick man recover. He lies on a stretcher in the background while a group of people dance around him.

This procedure is still in use today. Saunas are just updated sweat lodges, and they can be found in many different spas and resort areas around the world today. A number of different veterans' hospitals in the United States, including ones in South Dakota, Minnesota, and Utah, offer sweat lodges for use by Native American veterans.

Another technique used in different tribes was sand paintings. Holy men of the tribe would make a round bed of sand on the floor of the main tepee or in the center of the village and then decorate it with various designs and symbols. The circle could be as little as one foot in diameter or as large as 20 feet. Color was added to the painting by using ground up charcoal, root bark,

> The Cheyenne and Kiowa medicine men were known to do simple *amputations* and surgery. They would close the open wound by using a wooden suction cup and melted buffalo *tallow*.

crushed flowers, and pollen. Complex designs were made, often taking hours. Researchers have listed over 500 different sand painting patterns that were used. Not a single design was written down. Instead, they were handed down from generation to generation of healers. Each design made, however, contained a deliberate mistake because the Indians believed only the Great Spirit could create something that was completely perfect.

The sick person would be placed in the middle of the sand painting circle, and the rest of the tribe would chant to help get rid of any evil spirits. The sand painting had to be scattered by sunset, however, to prevent evil spirits from seeing it and coming to cause trouble. The sand would be gathered and then blown back into the same wind from which it had come. For example, if the wind had been blowing east when the sand was collected, it would be returned to a wind blowing east.

What happened if you had a broken bone or a deep cut? For accidental injuries, Native Americans had other common-sense remedies. *Abscesses* and *boils* were lanced or cut off; arrows and bullets were removed, if possible. Wounds were sewn up, and snakebites were sucked to remove the poison. The Ojibwa tribe would heat birch bark

47

NATIVE AMERICAN LIFE

Holding their weapons and wearing buffalo skins acquired from previous hunts, a group of Mandan hunters perform a buffalo dance. The dance was intended to summon buffalo herds. It was believed that if a medicine man blessed the hunt and the dance was performed correctly, the hunt would successful.

and use it to bind a broken bone. As it cooled, it would harden and form a cast. Sore or rotten teeth were knocked out with a hammer.

If you like to dance and move around, the method of healing that you might have liked best would have been the stomp dance. This dance was a fun way to help people feel better. Many Indians felt that the body must be in harmony with the earth and nature, and one way to do this was through dancing. The exercise of it would bring the soul closer to the Great Spirit, lessen stress, and make the person feel more whole.

If the main thing bothering a person was nightmares, the solution was found in the

> The Navajo believed the earth had the power to drain energy from things, so during a healing ceremony, they would make sure that all the tools, herbs, and baskets stayed up off the ground.

Canadian and North American Indians' dream catcher. Legend states that a Sioux woman once had a child who couldn't sleep due to bad dreams. The mother went to Old Spider Woman for advice. She was told to make a circle out of willow branches and weave the inside with cotton threads. This net would trap all the nightmares, but allow the good dreams to filter through.

Life changed dramatically for the Indians during the late 19th century, when many tribes lost battles, land, and basic rights to the white men's armies. By 1889, when Thomas Jefferson Morgan, the government's Commissioner of Indian Affairs, stated that, "The Indian must *conform* to 'the white man's ways,' peaceably if they will, forcibly if they must," it spelled the end of many centuries-old traditions. Rituals and sacred ceremonies were deemed against the law. Medicine men and shamans were arrested and put in jail.

Almost 100 years later, as Native Americans have finally begun to regain the respect they'd once lost in this country, their important traditions are coming back. Reservations are growing, and with them, the rich legacy of shamans, natural medicine, and belief in the power of nature. S

49

NATIVE AMERICAN LIFE

Chronology

1492 Christopher Columbus lands in the Americas; at this time, it is estimated there are more than 9 million Native Americans living in North America.

1524 Explorer Giovanni da Verrazzano gives the earliest account of coastal Indians and offers the first real description of their lifestyles.

1564–1565 Artist Jacques Le Moyne paints the first portraits of Native Americans.

1579 Sir Francis Drake visits the Miwok Indians in California.

c. 1590 The Iroquois League of Five Nations (Cayuga, Mohawk, Onondaga, Oneida, and Seneca) is created.

1609 New York Indians are introduced to firearms and alcohol by Henry Hudson.

1621 Native Americans and Pilgrims make a promise to be peaceful and helpful to each other.

1626 Governor Peter Minuit buys Manhattan Island from the Algonquian Indians for about $24.

1637 The Pequot War is fought.

1643 *A Key into the Language of America*, the first Native American-English dictionary is published in London.

1675 The English organize a board of commissioners for Indian Affairs.

1675–1678 King Philip's War between the British and most of the New England tribes is fought.

1680 New Mexico Pueblo Indians rebel against Spanish rule.

1689–1697 King William's War is fought, and the Iroquois side with the English against the French.

1692 Spaniards succeed in their conquest of the Native Americans of New Mexico.

1703 The Apalachee Indians, allies of the Spaniards, are killed in the Apalachee War.

1722 The Tuscarora Indians become members of the Iroquois Confederacy.

1730 Cherokee Indian chiefs make a pact with King George II.

1751 The Piman Indians stage an uprising against the Spaniards.

1754–1763 The French and Indian War is fought.

1755 Power is taken away from the Albany Board of Indian Commissioners.

1763 King George III issues a statement declaring that Indian country is all land west of the Appalachian Mountains.

1778 The first treaty between the United States and Delaware Indians is signed.

1779 General John Sullivan destroys much of the Iroquois.

1790–1799 Acts involving Native Americans become federal law; enforcement is placed in the hands of a department within the War Department.

1799 Handsome Lake, a Seneca chief, begins a new Indian religion known as the "long house" religion. It is still practiced today.

1813 Tecumseh, a Shawnee Indian leader, is killed.

1824 A Bureau of Indian Affairs is officially set up within the War Department.

1835 A policy of removing Native Americans from their lands in the southeast begins, and the Five Civilized Tribes (Cherokees, Seminoles, Creeks, Choctaws and Chickasaws) are moved along the "Trail of Tears" to Indian Territory in present-day Oklahoma.

1835–1842 The Seminole War is fought, and Chief Osceloa is killed.

1853–1857 The United States acquires 157 million acres of Indian land through treaties.

1862 The Sioux Indians stage an uprising in Minnesota and are forced to flee west.

1867 A peace commission is set up by the government to end war with the Native Americans.

1868 The Navajo Indian Reservation is created.

1871 Congress passes a law that forbids any more negotiations between Indians and the U.S.

1876 The Battle of the Little Big Horn is fought.

1877 The Nez Percé Indians lose a war with the U.S. and are sent to Oklahoma.

1879 The first Indian boarding schools are started.

1890 The Ghost Dance movement becomes popular among Plains Indians, and the massacre at Wounded Knee occurs.

1917 The Papago Indian Reservation in Arizona is established.

1922 The Pueblo Indians unite into the All Pueblo Council.

1934 The Indian Reorganization Act is passed.

1944 The National Congress of American Indians is established.

2003 Recent census figures indicate there are more than 3 million Native Americans living in the United States and Canada.

Glossary

abscess a localized collection of pus surrounded by inflamed tissue.

amputation the removal of a limb of the body.

annual a plant that completes its life cycle in one growing season.

antibiotic a substance produced by a microorganism used to inhibit or kill another microorganism.

antidote something that stops a poison from working.

arthritis inflammation of the joints.

boil a localized swelling and inflammation of the skin resulting from infection in a skin gland.

conform to comply with a fixed standard, regulation, or requirement.

congestion blocked up, not allowing movement through.

coniferous a type of tree that produces cones.

diagnosis the cause or nature of a patient's health problem or disease.

dilute to make weaker by adding water or another liquid.

enlightenment understanding of some new information.

fasting going without food of any kind for a period of time.

gourd a hard-rinded inedible fruit often used for ornament.

hallucination something not real that is seen in the mind of a person, often under the influence of drugs.

herb an aromatic plant used for its medicinal properties.

initiate somebody who has been recently admitted to an organization or religion after participating in a ritual or ceremony.

liniment a liquid or semiliquid substance applied to the skin as a soothing agent.

malachite a green compound that is used as a decorative stone and a source for copper.

malaria a serious disease that people can get from mosquito bites.

meditation a period of thinking very deeply about something, or a form of mental exercise.

ointment a smooth, greasy substance used on the skin to soothe soreness or itchiness, help wounds heal, or make skin softer.

perennial a plant that lives and flowers for more than two years.

peyote a globe-shaped cactus native to Mexico and the southwestern United States that has small rounded nodules, called buttons, which contain mescaline, a hallucinogenic drug.

pictographs written symbols used to record important information.

poultice a moist or damp pack made of herbs and other ingredients and placed on a wound or painful area of the body for healing.

rheumatism a disease that causes the joints and muscles to become swollen, stiff, and painful.

ritual a set of actions that is always performed in the same basic way, often as part of a religious ceremony.

scurvy a disease caused by lack of vitamin C.

shaman a Native American leader who acted as a go-between for the physical world and the spirit world, and who was said to have powers such as prophecy and healing.

smallpox a highly contagious disease caused by a virus and marked by high fever and the formation of inflamed areas of the skin filled with pus.

supernatural the realm of magic or other things that cannot be explained by natural laws.

tallow solid fat used chiefly in soap, candles, and lubricants.

trance in a conscious state, but not aware of what is going on around you.

vision quest a personal spiritual search undertaken by an adolescent Native American boy in order to learn, by means of a trance or vision, the identity of his guardian spirit.

Further Reading

Ake, Anne. *The Apache*. San Diego: Lucent Books, 2000.

Debelius, Maggie. *The American Indians: The Spirit World*. Alexandria: Time-Life Books, 1992.

Erdoes, Richard, and Alfonso Ortiz, eds. *American Indian Myths and Legends*. New York: Pantheon, 1984.

Glatzer, Jenna. *Native American Festivals and Ceremonies*. Philadelphia: Mason Crest, 2003.

Goodchild, Peter. *Survival Skills of the North American Indians*. Chicago: Chicago Review Press, 1999.

Hardin, Terri, ed. *Legends and Lore of the American Indians*. New York: Barnes and Noble Books, 1993.

Hoxie, Frederick E. *Encyclopedia of the North American Indians*. New York: Houghton Mifflin, 1996.

Kallen, Stuart A. *Native American Chiefs and Warriors*. San Diego: Lucent Books, 1999.

Lassieur, Allison. *Before the Storm: American Indians Before the Europeans*. New York: Facts on File, Inc, 1998.

Marcello, Patricia C. *The Navajo*. San Diego: Lucent Books, 2000.

Moulton, Candy. *Everyday Life Among the American Indians*. Cincinnati: Writer's Digest Books, 2001.

Owusu, Heike. *Symbols of Native America*. New York: Sterling Publishing, 1997.

Press, Petra. *Indians of the Northwest: Traditions, History, Legends and Life*. Milwaukee: Gareth Stevens Publishing, 2000.

Pritzker, Barry M. *A Native American Encyclopedia: History, Culture, and Peoples*. New York: Oxford University Press, 2000.

Rice, Earle Jr. Life *Among the Great Plains Indians*. San Diego: Lucent Books, 1998.

Sita, Lisa. *Indians of the Great Plains: Traditions, History, Legends and Life*. Milwaukee: Gareth Stevens Publishing, 2000.

———. *Indians of the Northeast: Traditions, History, Legends and Life*. Milwaukee: Gareth Stevens Publishing, 2000.

———. *Indians of the Southwest: Traditions, History, Legends and Life*. Milwaukee: Gareth Stevens Publishing, 2000.

Staeger, Rob. *Native American Religion*. Philadelphia: Mason Crest, 2003.

Streissguth, Thomas. *The Comanche*. San Diego: Lucent Books, 2000.

Williams, Colleen Madonna Flood. *Native American Family Life*. Philadelphia: Mason Crest, 2003.

Internet Resources

http://www.kstrom.net/isk/food/plants.html
This web site provides a list of Native American herbs and plant remedies.

http://www.nlm.nih.gov/exhibition/if_you_knew/if_you_knew_04.html
This site gives the views of 19th-century doctors toward Native American medical practices.

http://www.healing-arts.org/mehl-madrona/mmtraditionalpaper.htm
This site provides a modern-day look at the effectiveness of Native American medicine as part of a total healing program.

http://www.ilt.columbia.edu/k12/naha/natime.html
This is a timeline of Native American history and includes information on various events.

http://www.angelfire.com/mo/nativeamericanjrnl/page6.html
This is a Web site that provides a wide variety of Native American quotes on a range of subjects.

NATIVE AMERICAN LIFE

Index

NATIVE AMERICAN LIFE

Picture Credits

Contributors

Dr. Troy Johnson is a Professor of American Indian Studies and History at California State University, Long Beach, California. He is an internationally published author and is the author, co-author, or editor of fifteen books, including *Contemporary Political Issues of the American Indian* (1999), *Red Power: The American Indians' Fight for Freedom* (1999), *American Indian Activism: Alcatraz to the Longest Walk* (1997), and *The Occupation of Alcatraz Island: Indian Self-Determination and the Rise of Indian Activism* (1996). He has published numerous scholarly articles, has spoken at conferences across the United States, and is a member of the editorial board of the journals *American Indian Culture and Research* and *The History Teacher.* Dr. Johnson has served as president of the Society of History Education since 2001. He has been profiled in *Reference Encyclopedia of the American Indian* (2000) and *Directory of American Scholars* (2000). He has won awards for his permanent exhibit at Alcatraz Island; he also was named Most Valuable Professor of the Year by California State University, Long Beach, in 1997. He served as associate director and historical consultant on the PBS documentary film *Alcatraz Is Not an Island* (1999), which won first prize at the 26th annual American Indian Film Festival and was screened at the Sundance Film Festival in 2001. Dr. Johnson lives in Long Beach, California.

Tamra Orr is a full-time professional writer for many national magazines and the author of two books for children and two books on home schooling. She has been married for 20 years and is the mother of four. She believes that her children teach her more every single day.